A Planetful of Poems

A collection of poetry

About the world around us and inside us

WITH LOVE
x

by
Andrew Hawkins

After my previous collection of poetry 'Everything's Within' I decided to challenge myself to write poems about things around the world, from the atoms within all matter, to the mountains we climb.

This book is a mixture of these poems and my usual style of positive poetry, touching upon the infinite connections between all things. There are also a few poems that relate to times gone by, myths, dreams and memories.

I hope you enjoy the poems as much as I enjoyed writing them.

I am so thankful for coming into existence, even if it is for just a fleeting moment in the grand scale of unfathomable time.

We are all incalculable miracles that have been brought into consciousness. And it's a joy to be able to share my words with you.

1. Wishing Well
2. Gold
3. Affinity
4. Raise the Sails
5. Shanties
6. The Lighthouse
7. Shores of Love
8. The Storm
9. Shipmates
10. From the Depths
11. Tidal Waves
12. Flowers & Skulls
13. Dust
14. Ballroom Dreams
15. Dance
16. Energy
17. Feelings
18. Whispers
19. Imagine
20. Heartbeat
21. Echoes
22. Nature's Radio
23. Meadows of Tomorrow
24. Phenomenon
25. Clouds
26. Fly High
27. Unseen
28. Aura
29. Bright
30. Moonbeams
31. Linger
32. Moments
33. Hand on Your Heart
34. It Lives
35. Prevail
36. The Waterfall
37. Light & Shade
38. The Sculptor
39. Aurora
40. Divinity
41. Sunset
42. Space Rockets
43. Soar
44. Gaea
45. Epipelagic
46. The Sea
47. To & Fro
48. Breathe
49. Comfort
50. Doorways
51. Haunted
52. Ghosts
53. Midnight
54. Decay
55. Memories
56. Offspring
57. Afterlife
58. Ashes
59. Mountains
60. Reservoirs
61. Rhythm
62. Conquer
63. Discover
64. Equality
65. King & Queen
66. Motherland
67. Secret Place
68. The Flower
69. The Bee
70. Seduction
71. Senses
72. Light
73. Open Up
74. Pathways
75. Spiral
76. Carefree
77. Back Home
78. City of Trees
79. Mother Nature
80. Fragments
81. Spectral
82. Puddles
83. Reflecting
84. The Sun
85. Align
86. Forever
87. Nirvana
88. Other Side
89. Lucky Stars
90. Soul Song
91. The Moon
92. The Night
93. Daylight
94. Sounds
95. Protégés
96. Exquisite
97. Gaiety
98. Masquerade
99. Sail
100. Swim
101. Tangled
102. Break Free

Wishing Well

Throw your last coin in the wishing well
Breathe in the vaporous morning mist
Hear the splash down below
Feed your imagination's wanderlust

Close your eyes and let go
Get carried away on the meadow scent
Aged bark and weeping willow
Feel your soul in full ascent
Soaring to the clouds

Keep those eyelids closed now
You're free from all the crowds
You're one with everything
Now cry your glee out loud

Gold

His gold was green

A forest of dreams

Treasure that could not be measured

A place of nature

Away from the machines

Where everything was equal

And balance was restored

Each leaf a tiny painting

For his imagination to explore

Affinity

Wandering along the shorelines of infinity
Everything is ancient
But somehow new to me

As I grasp at the grains of sand
They cascade back
Into the tides of destiny

I watch the moonrise
Reflecting in the sea
As crashing waves play a deathless melody

I see the sparkling sea
Like a mirror to my soul
And I get lost in the affinity

Raise the Sails

Free my anchors

Raise my sails to the sky

With a whole ocean to explore

These feelings multiply

Dreamlike waves crashing blue

Every second this freedom burns

My solitude dwells here with you

Between weathered bow and shabby stern

Shanties

We sail on the oceans of time

Weaving through the flotsam and jetsam

Rippling within our minds

Fragments of the past

Jumbled with dreams of the future

We bellow inside "avast!"

Longing to reach that treasure we bear

Many batten down the hatches

These old sea dogs despair

Ahoy! Let yourself sink beneath the threshold

Where you'll hear shanties that shimmer

And find loot more precious than gold

The Lighthouse

The tall tower protruding observes
Whilst wails of constant winds
Are deadened by the waves
Crashing abundantly aground

But glimpsed through whimsical sea mist
The light cleaves through in rays
To give hope to who are lost
And to guide ashore their days

Shores of Love

The Earth is an island
And space is the sea
And we find ourselves
Such versatile creatures
Amongst this island's
Incalculable features
There is so much treasure
But the biggest riches
Cannot be measured
As they lie within our souls
For we are the inventions
Of energy aeons old
And we are worth so much more
Than our weight in gold
We are the pinnacle of existence
Across space and distance
So let's look deep inside
And let our shores of love unfold

The Storm

We spent our days on salty seas

Cutting through the waves

Our destiny crashing beneath the keel

This old brig had seen better days

And came the day of that mighty storm

That crept upon us from the east

To send us to the depths below

Descending down like leaves

Shipmates

Let's eliminate

Fear and hate

Lead our lives lovingly without depression

Let's celebrate

And liberate

Free everyone from oppression

We are all shipmates

On Mother Earth

So let's advocate

For a better world

Let's make it our obsession

From the Depths

I accept I am a vessel

Containing the energy of a billion years

I feel the sense of purpose

That courses through my veins

I feel your presence from the depths

To the edge of my senses

I feel your love expressing itself

Longing to connect with all

I take your hand in the endlessness

So together we can stand tall

Tidal Waves

Fill the barren lands of your mind

With tidal waves of seeds

So flowers bloom endlessly

Across the synapse seas

Bear the fruits of what is grown

Inside your skull which feeds your soul

Forget the pain that once was known

And live in love as you grow old

Flowers & Skulls

I see flowers through the skulls

Rusty nails and empty holes

Rotting wood by the stream

Where mushrooms unfold

I sense auras of stories untold

Of souls now lost to dreams

Memories scattered into the soil

Of love, compassion and toil

Nothing but seeds in the scenery

Feeding the flowers and greenery

Dust

The potions and pills
Sit gathering dust
On the windowsill
The rain outside
Never seems to subside
As the cobwebs in the corner
Gather droplets like pebbles
The carriage clock
Ticks its last tock
As time fades away
The pictures on the wall
Now faces without names
The upside down book
On the arm of the chair
A half-finished story
Gone with the soul
That once sat there

Ballroom Dreams

In an empty ballroom

Memories of swirling dresses

Settled dust permeates

Bow ties and cocktails

Chandeliers up high

Cigar smoke undulates

The drunken laughter of camaraderie

Echoes freely

As the big band bombilates

An era lost in time

But alive in my mind

Ghostly dreams I venerate

Dance

When your life becomes a chore
Your soul is not alive
Anymore
When your days just feel the same
And all you can do is blame
You're disconnected
You need to take a look inside
Find the beat within and
Thrive
Strive to be the best of you
Your version true
And release your inner wild
That of which has always been
Our true nature
That is dampened by the mire
Of everyday propensities
To numb us and divide
Us from who we are
And the Universe inside
So take my hand
And dance with me
Back into the world
Within you and around us all
Where love is felt
In everything
Through connections
Oh so grand

Energy

Do not let thoughts tear you asunder
Try making the space for joy and wonder

Let the woes spill from your mind
Leaving nothing but joy of the unbridled kind

Let this wonder fill up your heart
And see your life like a work of art

See yourself for the magic you are
Pure universal energy born from the stars

Feelings

I can hear your feelings

Ever healing

When your heart takes over your mind

And you set yourself free

Like an ember from the fire

To live in truth that drowns the lies

With our hearts leading the way

We come together

With our hopes and dreams aligned

Whispers

Eternal whispers in your eyes

That fear can't disguise

The reflection of the moonlight

That bounces back into mine

Our souls cohere in the night

The autumn rain cools our skin

But cannot dampen our passion within

This furnace of love deep in our core

As we whirl in the scent of sweet petrichor

Imagine

Could you imagine?

If the sound of our hearts

Was the only thing we could hear

Everything would become clear

Could you imagine?

If the only thing we could see

Was the love of energy

We could all unite

And dance in harmony

Heartbeat

The immortal presence of the Universe's energy

Sings within your soul

And will guide you through the chaos

From childhood to old

It's there inside your heartbeat

It echoes through your senses

Of a billion vibrations

So let go of apprehension

And be the vessel of energy you are

With this knowledge you'll go far

Echoes

We don't know exactly

How our future

Is affected by the past

But we do know

That what we do right now

Can last

So let's build a world on kindness

That echoes freely to our children

So they can create even greater things

In a world of love and freedom

Nature's Radio

The spirit of the air

Fulfils my lungs

As the sound of the rain

Like a million tiny drums

Plays nature's radio

I dance to the sounds

With freedom between my toes

As the beautiful light of day

Creates shapes with my shadow

I splash through the puddles

And kick up miniature rainbows

Meadows of Tomorrow

Take me to the meadows of tomorrow

Where we drown in peace

Beyond the ashes of sorrow

Where our joy is unbridled

And our love unrivalled

No longer living in fear

For we see each other

As sister & brother

No separation in our hearts

Living in each moment

Our lights glowing bright

Like breathtaking art

Phenomenon

You are a phenomenon

A star's energy

Living on and on

A wonderful fusion

Of atoms and time

Existing on a planet in space

How prodigiously sublime

And I get to share this place with you

And well, that's just divine

Clouds

Water containers in the sky

Some will rain

And some roll by

Some are fluffy

And some be flat

Some wisp around mountains

And others grow fat

I love all the clouds

In all of their forms

And when the rain comes down

I'll dance in the storms

Fly High

Couldn't find my way home

Couldn't find my way inside

But then the silence of love

Took my hand

And showed me how to survive

To thrive

To feel truly alive

By letting go of all the thoughts

And now in purity

I fly high

Unseen

Somewhere in the unseen

Is a realm that holds our dreams

A spectrum beyond imagination

Where all is lush and green

A sanctuary just beyond our senses

Where peace is relentless

Where the chaos turns into rapture

And there our youthfulness recaptured

Aura

Let me get lost in the wilds of your heart

And wade in the passion of your aura

Let me stay just a little longer

And drown in your song amidst the flora

Bright

If you stray

I will be here

To hold your hand

Every day

If I cry

It's just because

I sense your pain

And want to help you fly

I will see it through

And remind you of your light

As we place our hands together on your heart

To let your love shine bright

Moonbeams

I whisper to the mighty sea

To take me to my destiny

I chase waves like they're dreams

And as I sail my ship at night

The only light that guides me

Are these rippling moonbeams

For the power of the ocean

I hold in esteem

Linger

Wilted rivers dry up the sea

But the fervour of existence

Still reigns inside of me

Although my time is fading out

My heart still beats

Beyond confusion and doubt

My memories will linger on

In my family and friends

Even when my light goes out

My flame will never end

Moments

When I'm gone

My words will live on

So I write from my heart

In the hope it makes you strong

I want you to live to your fullest

For you are only you once

Treasure each moment

As if it was your last

Love the world around you

And live a life unsurpassed

Hand on Your Heart

I don't know how to tell you

But I'll try and I'll try

You come from stars above

Up there in the sky

You're a piece of star stuff

Brought to life

So please join me

And put your hand on your heart

And feel all strife

Wash away

Leaving you pure

Knowing that this truth will suffice

It Lives

It lives

Inside us

And around us

It lives

In the empty spaces

And solid rocks

It lives

In the air

And in the sea

It thrives everywhere

Beyond what we can see

It lives

Does the Universe's energy

Prevail

You'll find me

Beneath the trees

Prevailing so elegantly

Glowing in the radiance

Of a million golden leaves

A place my heart will never leave

For the crisp colourful carpet

Will soon decay into the soil

Feeding colours to come

The beautiful flowers

Yet sprung

The Waterfall

Cascading from the mountain tops
Rushing wild water flows
Horizontal; vertical
The direction goes

Tumbling over ancient rocks
Crashing into inviting pools
Like a big white ribbons
Feeding rivers down below

Light & Shade

Take my hands

As we dance and sway

Here beneath

The waterfall's cascade

Look into my eyes

So we can see

Our perfect selves

In harmony

Infinite reflections

Of light and shade

Countless connections

That have no age

For we are love

And we are unafraid

The Sculptor

How bewitching the wind

The invisible sculptor

Shaping trees on a whim

Creating waves on land

Eloquently across meadows

Whilst whipping up storms out to sea

From whispering zephyr to tumultuous tornado

Constantly creating artistic mastery

Aurora

Solar winds
Mingling in the sky
Playing in magnetic fields
To treat our human eyes

In the upper atmosphere
Colliding with atoms of gas
Creating magical colours
In streaks they do amass

Aurora Borealis
Giving Earth a spectral kiss
Like an artist with a brush
Painting Earth from the abyss

Divinity

Take me to places I've never been

Let me see wonder I've never seen

Let me see life in each moment new

Let me live abundantly and true

To absorb all the divinity

And appreciate this essence

So I can show others this purity

To live in freedom and coexistence

Sunset

I went down to the river's edge

That day

And saw the evening glow

Glimmer across the surface

And I was thankful and at one

For this short but beautiful life

As I listened to the birds in the trees

Sing a grateful song to the setting sun

Space Rockets

All the ways

We spend our days

Working

To put profits

In the bigwig's pockets

We could instead

Be exploring the vastness of the dark

In space rockets

Learning about everything we are

From the distant stars

If we could use all the money spent on wars

We would already be beyond mars

Discovering new secrets

And expanding our hearts

Soar

I'm floating

As my planetary anchors

Unshackle

For my purpose now

Is shifting

The Universe is calling me

To return whence I came

My energy

The stuff of stars

Must disperse back

Into the Cosmos

And my soul

Will soar again

Gaea

The grass protrudes between my toes

As I connect with Earth

Letting me know I am loved

And reminding me of this connection

That has been here since my birth

For without Gaea

I would not be

So I thank her endlessly

And in her honour

I live my life with mirth

Epipelagic

We all breathe the same air

That's why I care

We inhale the same treasure

And it really is no small measure

That we've come to be

As we live amongst this magic

Since we emerged from the epipelagic

With no fear

Millions of years ago

So why don't we

Cry happy tears

And try to live in harmony

The Sea

We cast ourselves in boats to sea

To see what waits on distant shores

Unsure of what treasures we may unearth

With mirth we ride the ocean tide

And abide the ocean rules

To discover lands brand new

In joy and laughter

Drunk from the ocean dew

To & Fro

There's a place inside
That all of us can find
It lies within our hearts
When we escape our minds

And then we realise
Our paths are realigned
Our souls all shine together
And we're no longer blind

And in these fields we glow
Swaying to and fro
Living life in harmony
And letting our dreams grow

Breathe

Settle down

Breathe

There is nothing on your shoulders

The only woes live in your thoughts

And they don't help you in the now

They just cause aggravation

So rise above them

Be ever present

With your presence

Which will help you with each situation

Comfort

I've been chasing spirits

Of the person you once were

Trying to hold off solitude

Against the wrath of time

Your memories trapped in photographs

The faces lose their names

All I can do is hold your hand

And be your comfort in the dark

Doorways

Under the branches

Puddles and leaves collide

With birdsongs in my ears

I inhale the beautiful scents

That nature provides

The sunbeams perforate between the leaves

I see wonders in the glint

Casting patterns of light and shadows

Between tree trunks like infinite doorways

That lead home with every footprint

Haunted

Our pulse is haunted

By the chaos of the stars

A flow unfiltered

Living celestial memoirs

These atoms now form

As earthly avatars

With complex purity

Beating out from our hearts

Ghosts

We play hosts

To timeless ghosts

Reverberating across time

The souls of the Universe

Vivid and sublime

Energy born from the stars

Magic, is what we are

So treasure the fire inside

And live your life with verve

There's no need to hide

Midnight

I find myself dancing

Here beneath the trees

Doused in the moonlight

Toes skipping through the leaves

My breath like tiny clouds

Captured in the midnight breeze

My soul connected to everything

My heart beating strong and free

Decay

The shallow water in the well
Gets coated with autumn leaves
The decaying bucket turns a brownish green
Damp and teeming with mushrooms
As the handles rust in the breeze
The stones remain a stubborn grey
They've stood the test of time
The nearby shack now overgrown
Which nature has come to own
Just remnants and trinkets left
Of a simple but happy life
Living at one with the meadow
And gone are the evening fire pits
Flickering the trees yellow

Memories

I believe in a brighter future

Where all our hopes come to fruition

And our dreams become a reality

Where we all live as one

In unison and love

As we conquer our fears and insecurities

For the peace we all yearn for

So they are nothing but forgotten memories

Offspring

I wish I could abduct your tears

And take away the pain

Only to give them back

When you're ready to cry tears of joy

When you realise the beauty

Of your existence

Is connected to everything

For you are the Universe's

Conscious offspring

Afterlife

When I'm laid deep in the earth

I will speak on through the trees

My life will bring visitors back

Who will speak softly and lay their wreaths

And on my soul will sing

Permeating through the ground

Feeding the worms

Which then feed the birds

So I can fly freely on their wings

Ashes

Why do we let the demons feast
On our inner fears
Whilst we look to blame ourselves
For they are one and the same
The demons are us
And we them
The trick is how they're slain
We no longer give them power
We let go of our attachments
And let the flowers grow
Within the space we create
Let love thrive from the ashes

Mountains

Primordial concoctions

Forged long ago

From shifts and eruptions

Came mountaintop constructions

Now places of awe

For humans to conquer

We play with death

And ever changing weather

To catch our breath

At the peaks of these summits

To feel more alive than ever

Reservoirs

With my hands held high

Towards the sky

I cry

A thousand tears of joy

Embracing my fleeting moment of existence

In this Universe

Of stars

We are what we're made of

Universal conscious reservoirs

Rhythm

We are the reality definers

With eternity inside us

Conscious dimensional beings

Gaining wisdom through thinking and seeing

Making connections to all around

Attuned to our senses

Creating new art and sounds

We've even worked out how to fly

Us creatures on the ground

For knowingly or not

We are reaching for the stars

The very life givers

Who brought rhythm to our hearts

Conquer

The fear in my mind was my demise

But in a moment of silence

I heard the love in my heart

And still to this day

I rise

For as long as The Earth

Is warmed by The Sun

I will endeavour

To pass my love on

So we can all conquer fear

One beat at a time

Discover

Stop running

And dive right in

To discover everything

Stop hiding

And delve inside your heart

To reveal the answers

You were avoiding

Time will only fade

So face your fears with conviction

So you can overcome them steadfastly

And live a life free of friction

Equality

I wish to see peace across the Earth

Our home we should cherish

Equality for each and all

And do away with prejudice

To give life a new lease

Let the children be free

Where we can teach them peace

And to live in harmony

King & Queen

The forest is our limousine

With me its king and you my queen

A red carpet of leaves

Let's see where it leads

I'm sure everything here in nature

Will be far from pristine

But that's fine with me

Let's dance here a while

And get muddy and green

Motherland

The trees and hills are nature's pills

To raise us off our knees

To rid us of this disease

Of oppression

Force feeding us depression

Keeping us trapped in mental boxes

Through manipulation and suggestion

Making us feel we're separate from each other

Dividing us through politics & colour

So let's all take each other's hands

And walk together

Back into our motherland

Secret Place

I found a secret place inside

And decided to share it in a poem

To let everyone know it's in them too

We are all the Universe self-knowing

We cloud this fact with woes and worry

But if we just breathe

And realise

The miracle of being alive

We can wash the worries away

And live at one with everything

Every day

The Flower

Friends of the insects

Drinkers of light

Pleasant of smell

A visual delight

Nectar they give

So insects can live

But hitch a ride

To spread pollen wide

Petals they flout

Abundant in colour

Mother Earth is quite lucky

To be home of the flower

The Bee

Black and yellow

Buzzing navigator

Fuzzy fellow

Petal inspector

Flower pollinating

Nectar collector

Hexagonal maker

Honey creator

The humble bumble

Connector of nature

Seduction

The Seduction of Nature

And all of its features

Sings to my heart

Through rivers and creatures

I long to live forever

Upon mountains and under trees

Admiring the colours of leaves

And every type of weather

Senses

What are sounds?

If not for ears

To hear the raindrops splash like tears

What are sights?

If not for eyes

To see the colours change in the sky

What are smells?

If not for noses

To succumb to scents like summer roses

What are feelings?

If not for souls

To keep us connected as we grow old

Light

With eyes like galaxies

We bear witness to the journey

As receivers of the light

Like beacons to the stars

That transcend beyond our sight

Underneath our eyelids

We reminisce and coalesce

In dreamscapes we soar freely

Like satellites shimmering in starlight

Open Up

I couldn't recognise myself

When I lived with my guards up

What I didn't let in

Stumped my growth

Scared of letting in pain

I also left out love

I was killing myself slowly

Bitter and numb

But then I opened up

And my life again begun

Pathways

Turn every stone in your mind

And see what secrets you can find

Open new pathways to the heart

To give life new meaning

To see all the magic

And each moment as art

Dive inside the depth you

And get lost in the wonder

Let your infinite love break through

Spiral

Spiralling lights

Unearthly delights

Visions of lights in the dark

Bewildering cosmic delights

Warp speed infusion

Sparks of atomic surprise

Exploding into new dimensions

Vibrating new realms into our lives

Carefree

On the precipice of reality

Dancing carefree between the trees

Horizons blur into the distance

Roots entangle with the leaves

We meander through the forest

As we skip through rays of light

The shadows stretch peculiarly

As we dance the day into night

Back Home

Run away

Into nature

To find beauty

Go ever deeper

Beyond the branches

Where the oneness dwells

The birds sing the song of life

The leaves on the branches wave

Welcoming you back to your true home

Now sit here a while where you are never alone

City of Trees

Wandering down

To the city of trees

Beyond the urban grey

Where there are no leaves

Venturing in

To become one with it all

The nature in me

Sings at one with branches

Here I am complete

Where my heart dances

Mother Nature

We are all seedlings

Of Mother Nature's proceedings

Passing on her wisdom and traits

So future generations

Can adapt and mutate

And to think everything we are

Came from the stars

Epic alchemy is what we are

Fragments

We're all going back to where we came from

Parts of the fabric

Fragments of the one

We ride our paths from young to old

Passing on our atoms

When it's time to unfold

And our knowledge

The furnace we hold

That burns within us all

Will continue to bear our name

As you and I

The Earth and The Sun

Are one and the same

Spectral

The world is reversed

The mirror looks at you

Your dreamscape traverses

Into a realm of untold truths

The reflection gazing back

Is only there because of light

Presence comprehending itself

Through the spectral power of sight

Puddles

I see stars in puddles

Splashy pavement muddles

Dots of distant light at my feet

And I greet them in drunken joy

Not through inebriation

But through awe intoxication

That we come from their very cores

I see our creators

And I am filled with affection

At specs of light reflected

Reflecting

Atop the mountain high

Clouds beneath my feet

The world below so miniscule

The joy in each heartbeat

The crispy snow sparkling so bright

Reflecting the sun that shines above

I feel I can almost touch its surface

As it warms me with its love

The Sun

A sphere of hydrogen out in space
One of trillions, yet the one we grace

Creating purple haze in the evening
Sometimes it's red like the sky is bleeding

And the early risers may catch a glimpse
Of a golden glow, that can make you squint

Throughout the day rays pierce the clouds
And from its heat we are endowed

A plasma ball 93 million miles away
Yet with us each moment every day

Align

All I know

Comes to grow

As I absorb the world around me

Learning about its intricacies

I fathom out more about me

These deep connections entwine

Through the concept of time

My mind, heart and reality

All come to align

Forever

Can't you see?

This world belongs to you

This planet that you're a part of

Allow yourself to blend

Into all that you find true

Become one with all the energy

Listen to the beat in your heart

That connects everything back to the start

Listen to nature

Your forever friend

Letting you know to fear no end

The call of the wild resonates

Within our bones

The place where we come from

Our forever home

Nirvana

Bring me down to the valley of trees

Shake me to my core in the heavenly breeze

Show me where the stream meets the lake

Let me stay here and may I never wake

From this living dream of perfect peace

So I can stay in nirvana with no escape

Other Side

When I meet you on the other side

Beyond this mortal skin

Our energies will collide

From spirits released within

We'll traverse across the Universe

Becoming part of the great unknown

Finding ourselves amongst the shining stars

Back in our forever home

Lucky Stars

I am often overwhelmed

By the beauty of this world

And thank my lucky stars

That I am part of this realm

To be amongst the birds and bees

To saunter through forests

And feel connected to the trees

To dip my toes in rushing streams

And lose myself in the gentle breeze

Soul Song

This tapestry of you and me

Interwoven chemistry

A separation from the stars

To come back and reunite

In each other's hearts

This perfect fusion

That drowns out the mind's confusion

Keeps us whole

As we ride the waves of love

And sing the songs within our souls

The Moon

Be you full, or be you crescent
We gaze upon your glow so pleasant

Without you the world would be a different place
Without the pull of your gravity's embrace

The seasons wouldn't exist as we know them
Life would have gone so many different ways

So thank you moon for being with us
And lighting the night sky between our days

The Night

The lustrous puddle
Under the flickering streetlight
Charms me
As I saunter home
The buzzing silence
Whirs in my ears
My footsteps
On the pavement
The only sound
It's 1am
I don't want to go inside
When I can lie down in the wet grass
And ogle the stars
With my senses intensified

Daylight

You caught me in your cosmic rays

And I lingered there astonished

You shine relentlessly every day

Piercing the veil of trees above

To give light unto the forest

You spoil us with your daylight

For you show us all the colours

As we swim amongst the spectrums

And in your warmth we flourish

Like the insects and the flowers

Sounds

I heard your song and danced so effortlessly
The music seeped into my soul
Your sounds abundant radiated all around
I swam in the beauty
Although I drowned
In the wonder that is everything
From the subtle leaves
And birds calling
The raindrops splashing in the stream
These sounds keep playing like a dream
And even in the moments of silence
I could still hear
The wings of butterflies
Fluttering near
So I laid myself down
Into the ground
To become one
With all I've found

Protégés

We are all

Protégés

Of the Universe's

Magic ways

Portals for its consciousness

Breathing beings that exist

In a time and space dimension

Successes of its ascension

Exquisite

The day the fear stopped

Came out of the blue

It was in a moment of silence

I reconnected to the truth

This exquisite surprise

That the noise had disguised

A deep purpose swept through my soul

Reminding me I am part of everything

And it's only the voices in my head

That stopped me from realising

I am dynamic and whole

Gaiety

It's time to make amends

Cleanse your mind and soul

So your heart can grow

Be your own best friend

This can only serve you well

Until the very end

It will also leave happy trails

For others to follow

Your footsteps of happiness

In which their gaiety avails

Masquerade

As the snowflakes melt on our faces

We leave icy traces

Of enchanted wintry adventures

Fleeting footprints soon to fade

To give way

To the springtime masquerade

Of countless flowers emerging

Growing where we once danced

In a twinkling wonderland of escapades

Sail

The screams inside your head are silent
But the thoughts within them can be violent

So focus on the silent realm
And be the captain of your helm

Sail your thoughts into your heart
And watch the fear soon depart

Be the curator of your dreams
And drown in whispers beneath the screams

Swim

During the hazy wintery wilderness

I am warmed by a hearth

That burns deep in my heart

And guides me through the cold until spring

Watching the brittle branches swing in the wind

As if they were an orchestra

Waiting for their leaves to sing

These connections between the seasons

Make my soul swim

Tangled

Drowning in your deepest fears

Sinking further in

Any hope seemed futile

Tangled inside the chains in your mind

And your spirit capsized

But now you are unrestrained

Coming to realise

You were hiding behind a wall of lies

And now you live free

With your head held high

Break Free

You said it was over

But you're just a voice inside my head

I'll tell you it's over

There's no room left for your dread

I'm making room where there was heartache

Clearing delusions in my head

Breaking free from the illusions

To give myself a chance

I slipped through the grip of fear's fingers

And now I'm free to live and dance

Climbing

Climbing the ropes of cognizance

Grasping desires of somnolence

My body aging and scarred

Through tenacity I keep ascending

I gasp and smile through the pain

Knowing my journey is not in vain

I owe my ancestors of every ilk

For this glory of me

And I thank them wholeheartedly

Balance

He was raised by trees

Underneath the canopies

He grew to be at one

With everything from the owl's song

To the mushrooms between the leaves

He learned to only take what was needed

And to keep balance in the woods

Otherwise he knew one day

The owl would no longer sing

And the branches would succumb to silence

This much he understood

Nurture

Who knows what we're destined for?
But it seems to me
It's more and more
Our advancements
Have come on leaps and bounds
With new technologies
Made from elements found in the ground
We just have to do it with balance
Making sure we don't damage our ecosystem
And fail as a species
But I believe
With so much passion
And many brilliant minds
We can surely nurture
A beautiful path
Into the future

Playground

My love is not just mine
It's part of everything
It's care free and joyous
Like a child on a swing

My playground is the forest
My ocean is the sky
And my heart will sing endlessly
Until the day I say goodbye

Kids

We're all just grown up kids

Lost within the midst

Of modern society

Drunk on its distractions

Our new daily sobriety

So will you take my hand?

I'll lift you off your knees

Let's get back to where we belong

Frolicking between the trees

Revel

Slow down

Breathe

Take in what's all around

The colours

The smells

The sounds

Blend into it all

The infinite combinations

Of sensations

And revel

In this

Your divine

Perfect

Consciousness

Sway

Let's stay here in this moment

Forever

In this harmonious embrace

Beneath the branches

Let our hearts beat in rhythm

To the scintillating stars

And let the roots entwine

Around our feet

Our breath disperses into the night

As we sway together

Wholesomely

Under the moonlight

Creatures

All of this that surrounds me
Astounds me
The ocean
The sand
The wrinkles in my hands
Telling tales of time
In this reality so grand
The trees
And the lake
Greet me as I wake
The bags under my eyes
Are no surprise
From the late night
Gawking at the stars
In the hypnotising night sky
I wonder what becomes of them
And what children they will birth
Will they be so different to
Us creatures here on Earth?

Firmament

I went searching

For something I already owned

Deep with my flesh and bones

Was its lingering presence

But I kept trying to atone

Fighting this fear I fed myself

Until one day

I heard beyond the firmament

And I knew

I was never alone

Never Alone

You are never alone

You were born out of vastness

To be part of everything

The fact you can think these thoughts

Proves the infinite connections

That existed to give life to you

And even if you feel there are no humans that 'get you'

There are animals that will show you affection

Light that allows you to see your reflection

Trees that give you air

To let you breathe in perfection

Interlude

Here in the interlude

Between our rise and fall

We learn to take in what we are

Before our final call

We come to realise that we are energy

Vibrations brought to life

Trying to understand understanding

To exist as love beyond the strife

Passion

I see so many faces

Staring at newspaper pages

Drinking in the fear

Like it's going out of fashion

When it's mirthful

And far more exhilarating

To connect with the world around you

And fill up on radiant passion

Winning

Those tormentors they battered me

With their fists and their words

Leaving me shaking and bruised

But I listened to my heart

Tuned into what's pure

And told myself "you'll never lose"

So with new found courage

I drowned them with kindness

And made them reflect on their truths

Kindness

Speak your truth

Speak it proud

Sing if you have to

Make it loud

Let your heart

Be heard in your words

For others to cherish

Please don't be deterred

Use your voice for good

Empowerment and kindness

Like all of us should

Immensity

This is paradise

The same love I see within your eyes

Each freckle like a galaxy

Pulling me in and setting me free

As our fingers entwine

I have never felt so alive

In this timeless embrace

Sharing our little place

In the immensity of space

Benevolence

Sturdy in the ground

Yet submissive to the breeze

Roots far and wide

And an abundance of leaves

Oh how I love

The benevolence of trees

Watch them flourish

Grow lavish viridian shades

Then fade into saffron

When leaves crumple dead

Leaving the forest floor

A fiery gingerbread red

Autumn

These colours of death

From sweet autumnal breath

Invigorate me as I sway

In the seasonal scent of decay

Adorn

This existence is all for you

So chase your dreams

Do what you do

Live this one life

Pure and true

Be the joy of your beating heart

Leave no stone of your mind unturned

Express your love like a piece of art

So others can see the beauty you adorn

Spellbound

Spellbound and infatuated

By nature's sights and sounds

From sumptuous clouds up high

To roots sticking out of the ground

I get drawn in by the evening sunbeams

As my cheeks warm gently red

I gaze with ardour towards the horizon

As the birdsong fills my head

The Beckoning

There's a garden full of flowers

Calling your name

There's a rainbow in the sky

Showing its colours beyond the rain

There's a moon up above

To hug your soul at night

Glowing endlessly until the morning light

The dew drops on the dancing grass

Shimmer in the morning rays of the sun

Everything is beckoning you

To come and join the fun

Pleasure

The echo of our ancestors

Flows in our blood

That recognises toes in earth

And in the stars above

The sunrises of the seasons

The wind that sweeps the valleys

The waves that call for us to sail

Upon our salty galleys

To explore new land across the ocean

To find new fruits and treasure

With this sea air in our lungs

We sing heartily with pleasure

Romance

I've got that non-stop feeling

My arms held aloft

Reaching for the ceiling

Dreaming of flying off into space

To meet the stars

And embrace their grace

To soar across the great expanse

To see everything we are

In this cosmic romance

Song of the Night

Dip your toes in streams below

Quench sunlight through the trees

Inhale the fresh forest air

And sing into the breeze

Watch the evening mist pervade

As sun gives way to moon

The night sky returns your song

When stars above are strewn

Starlight

Sitting here in a shadow

In a crater on The Moon

Holding on for the starlight

I know it'll be here soon

To take solace in the knowledge

Across a million miles of space

That I'll soon be on my way home

To kiss your loneliness away

More Than Human

Every drop in the ocean
Is a tear the Universe cried
Every cloud formation
Is a timeless painting
And every starry night
Is a reminder
Of the glowing light
That shines deep within our core
We are more than human
The clues are everywhere
Bombarding our senses
With extravagance and flair
Telling us we are extraordinary
Magic beings breathing air
Contemplating our very existence
We are nature's billionaires

Crying

The Universe is crying out

Inside our hearts

It has done from the very start

To tell us that everything will be ok

For it beats in time with everything

From the ocean tides

And meadow winds

We are made from the same stuff

Us cosmic magical beings

Alzheimer's

Dear Mum

I know your memories are in there

But you can't hold onto them

As soon as one thing is remembered

It's gone and forgotten

I'll do everything I can

To keep your memories alive

That Alzheimer's has taken from you

I'll strive

And strive

And strive

Eternity

Let the fear be the fuel

To ignite the centre of you

To light the flame that sets you free

From the thoughts that keep you chained

Unrestrained, now in eternity

At one with all the elements

And everything around

Embrace your apogee

Fireflies

On my own

Sitting on a mossy log

As the owl song reverberates

Between the leaves gently dancing

The dots of distant city lights

Get lost amongst the fireflies

As The Moon passes by

The branches up high

I start to feel at home

Sitting here on this mossy log

As I realise I am never alone

Happy

Emerald leaves shroud the sky
But it doesn't leave me blue
Mossy paths guide the way
I wish you could be here too
Happy amber bees
Dance around my feet
Darting between violet shaded flowers
Going from foxglove to lavender on repeat
The sweet nectar
Fuels the gentle humming sound
As they cavort graciously
Just above the grassy ground
This precious act seems inconsequential
But it is oh so essential
Or ecosystems will break down

Delight

You know you've really got to live

Go out there

And give all that you can give

No need to sugar coat our stories

Just be free and live

We all end up with nothing

But can leave behind delight

So be the very best of you

And shine your love so bright

Extraordinary

Our spirits may fade away

But our songs go on forever

Reverberating down through generations

Reminding us we can always do better

So raise a glass for those now gone

They would want us to live merrily

And to cherish this precious life

So let's make it extraordinary

Fields

Take my hand and dance into the fields

Let's see together what freedom yields

Where we can live at one with nature's breath

And exist wholly in each moment until death

For we can be all the colours like flowers

The seeds in the ground and wings of a bee

We can bask in each morning sunrise

As we play in the shadows cast by the trees

Fortune

Our fortune

Our fable

Is that we are able

To love and to share

Inhaling this air

A gift from the trees

That makes everything thrive

So let's treasure this miracle

The fact we're alive

Potion

The ocean is a potion

That stirred us into motion

Now we roam on land

And build cities so grand

The daytime in our eyes

Reflects back blue skies

Across which we soar

But still we want more

As we gaze at night skies deep black

Filled with stars calling us back

Steel & Green

With steel we build
Our temples to the sky
Scraping the clouds
Like needles so high

But none will ever speak
The grace of trees below
The air that they give us
And the life they bestow

For I will always love trees
Because trees let me grow

The Architect

The universal architect

Through time

Has brought us here in flesh

Where we digress to muddle

Our minds with stories

And unnecessary struggles

That lead us away

From the simple truth

That we are pure vibrations

Of the architects intention

Vessels

The spools of reality

That split us apart

Are slowly weaving us

Back together

As the strings of time

Feed us thoughts

Of whom we are

And what we become

These vessels of energy

With the power to love

To spread joy and fun

Will You?

When I'm old
And not quite there
Will you still care?

When I'm receding
With wisps of grey hair
Will you still care?

When I'm not able
To make sense of things
Will you still care?

When I forget your face
And all we've done
Will you still care?

I always loved you
But when my mind forgets
Please still care

And when I'm not here tomorrow
Hold your hand to your heart
For I'll be in there

The Spider

Many fear me
But I mostly help
Clear your house of bugs

Can't they see?
The webs I build
Are created with such love

They even named the internet
After my creations
Surely that deserves
Just a little admiration

The Way Out

It's just another story we tell ourselves

When we listen to fear

From which the darkness dwells

The way out

Lies deeper inside

When we realise we are the void

Where the voices come from

We are that and more

The eternal expanse where we sing

Beyond the static and confusion

The place where energy begins

Betwixt

Let's get lost betwixt the trees

Let our soundtrack be the birds

And our scent be the flowers

Let us settle here forever

In these natural towers

Disperse

I float downstream

Like leaves that have fallen from above

Twirling where the water flows

In this sensuous dream

And when I reach the sea

I'll sink slowly through the fathoms

To disperse into the ocean floor

And return myself to me

Fire

We come from distant fires

We are an explosions desire

After billions of orbits

Around the sun

That fire inside us burns

As it yearns to learn

About itself

And in a moment of time

Through the cloud of malaise

We discover we are the flames

As we shed a teardrop of joy

That was born from the blaze

Esprit

Live your life with no remorse

Spread your love

And stay on course

For we are the ones

To echo our freedom and thoughts

Across the aeons

So the future souls

Can embrace our esprit

To be the very best beings

We can strive to be

Live On

It was so sad

That you had to go

But your memories live inside me

Each day

I see your face in the clouds

You live on in my energy

In tune with my soul

You make the grey skies blue

You give the colours truth

You give me reason for existing

You are the whispers between the seasons

Unison

We've come so far

As a species on a tiny planet

Spiralling round a distance star

So let's use this chance

To make good of our existence

For our love knows no distance

This energy vibrating in unison

Like true romance throughout all matter

Let's celebrate our souls and dance

Renaissance

A new renaissance

Waking up from the moonlight

Out from the shadows

A new world in sight

New found fledglings

Aiming for a target high

Tickets for a road to heaven

That can be found beneath the sky

Hate is washed away

When love is tasted in all its warmth

A billion hearts beat the dance of a song

To the creation of unison in astral form

Harvest

The songbird calls its morning call
As you sit lost by the television
Oceans flow back and forth
Shore to distant shore
Gentle strength flows over the face of Earth
The grace of nature's law
Wispy fields of golden weave
The falling leaves of season's exchange
Harvesting the yield
And discovering new change
When the sun shines in your eyes
It lights the fire of the place you live in
Reminiscent of all that is
Feelings of rearranging within
Take today in your hands
Feel it and go out and live it
Take today in your heart
Live proud and be it

Interwoven

We redefine to reconnect

To understand and reflect

Upon the lessons past and future fates

To live, learn and grow

Into the interwoven web of existence

In time with all that is

Points

Every point

Is the point of no return

So blossom in each moment

With all your love to burn

Leave nothing on the table

Live without regrets

Share the immensity of what you are

Be a mirror for others to reflect

So we all learn

From each other's fables

Beacon

I will always be the author of my life

The early chapters were full of strife

I've walked so many tracks

And fell between the cracks

But everything has led to this

A life where I've found who I am

For I am love

And now all I want to is be a beacon

And share this bliss

Being Human

I can't be the only one

Who finds this life so much fun

Although we have our woes

And tragedies

There's so much beauty

Out there to see

From thunderstorms

To deep blue seas

And all these feelings

That flow through our being

It's such a rush to be human

And when I leave this realm

I'll wish I could do it all again

Dreamers

Pushing the boundaries

We are the dreamers

And forefathers

Of fantasies

That we can bring to reality

These ideas that spill from our minds

Along with our passion and intensity

Can reshape our destiny

Embrace

Embrace your depths

These infinite tides

That keep you existing

Do you really need to hide?

When the waves inside

Are no different

Than those outside

For everything is energy

Connecting us all together

Like a magical tapestry

Tapestry

We are one

Only divided by the atoms

Of the suns we come from

We are all

Experiencing ourselves

As each other

Our actions all connected

Our hearts reflected

As we travel

Through the tapestry

Of reality

Virus

Don't let the virus divide us

Though it may manifest between us

Stay strong before the politics

We need not more conflict

Let us not argue amongst ourselves

Or leave nothing but empty shelves

Let us be here for each other

Even if it is from a distance

We are all in this together

Wealth

Rich are the poor
Who have no money
Who've made room in their hearts
For the love of the many

Poor are the rich
Who are blinded by false profit
For we all end up with nothing
No matter what is in our pockets

So let's share the love
And focus on our health
That is where we can thrive
In a world of true wealth

Wholeness

Serenity

Was never far from me

I always heard it calling

From inside

Wholeness

Was only hidden

Beneath the noise of thought

Until one day

There was nowhere left to hide

And now I swim

Through the treasure of life

In peace

With nature by my side

All In

The cards in your heart

Will only ever deal love

So if the joker in your head

Is filling you with dread

Fold that hand away

Now it's time to go all in

Taste that royal flush in your chest

Your winnings are there within

Divisions

I made the divisions in me

A reality

Not knowing that they were created

Merely by thinking I was not whole

The thoughts that came from the void

Creating imaginary trolls

In my skull

But I became aware of these invisible divisions

And showed them who's in control

Fortress

Once you find

Your fortress of freedom

In the middle of your kingdom

No fears will come within

For in this place

There is no trace

For your peace to crumble

As you can remain humble

Knowing there's no caprice

Where everything is your friend

And there's no beginning

Just a beautiful forever

With no end

Reshape

We've reshaped The Earth

So why don't we reshape our minds

To be more aligned

After all we call ourselves mankind

But we do not yet

Live up to our name

So let's no longer hang our heads

In shame

And realise our age old connection

With our planet

And treat her with all our affection

Mesmerised

Shivering in the heat of the sun

Mesmerised in the tantalising rays

Melting in its sweet caress

Admiring its power everyday

In love with a nuclear ball

Tied to its embrace

And gravity's pull

We spin round and round

Yet in its light we stand tall

Guise

We are the Universe

In human guise

A construct of atoms

In an earthly disguise

Flying through spacetime

On a watery sphere

Growing to know ourselves

In this time we adhere

Hills & Heather

I'm back where I belong

Singing my song

In the middle of nowhere

But it's somewhere I treasure

Amongst the hills and heather

With nothing to see

But miles and miles

Of landscape fantasy

Petals

Let the colours fall

Upon meadows and forest floors

Softly cascading fragments

Scented from the source

From blossom in full force

Wilted stems follow after

With roots entangled

To keep fear below

Petals dancing everywhere

Fuelling love to grow

Amplify

Come here with your fever

The ego deceiver

I'll wash over you with peace

And release you

Stay a while in my forest

And I promise

You'll lose the need to belong

In your headsong

It'll be replaced with glee

Joy and harmony

Beating from inside

Your love amplified

Gallery

The trees are my palace

For the forest is my kingdom

Ever present and alive

Where the birds sing their freedom

The leaves are my gallery

Guiding me through the seasons of time

I belong here beneath the canopies

Where the peace is so sublime

Step by Step

There are so many open roads

But all of them lead

Back home

To where we come from

We are all on the same course

Evolving to know ourselves

Step by step

We are all slowly

Returning to the source

Sunlight

We feel the sunlight

Pierce the veil of the Earth

Every morning an ambient glow

Every day like a new birth

Indebted to our golden star

Providing abundant life

Where there once was none

Warming the seas

And stirring the skies

Providing energy for plants

Who bequeath oxygen for life

The Ocean

I'd drink the ocean for me to get you
To feel your warm embrace
I'd drink the ocean just to be with you
To see that smile upon you face

I'd drink all the water on this sphere
And ground all the ships
But I'd replace the water with my tears
Once I've kissed your tender lips

Tempest

Be the river that feeds the trees

Which winds through forests and leads to sea

Be the nectar that fuels nature

And connects everything with ease

Be the silent oxygen that allows life to breathe

For you are the tempest of life

Be the energy that flourishes amongst it all

Give everything you have and thrive

Perfection

Did you know you're beautiful?

As perfect as can be

7 octillion atoms

Divine in form and so earthly

A creature worthy of any world

But so lucky to be here

So I'm honoured to share this place with you

Stardust that I revere

Gleam

I waded a little

Into your inviting shallows

But before I could realise

I was drowning in your depths

I got lost amidst the voices

All fighting for the stage

Telling me who and what I was

Trapped in my own cage

But one day I heard the silence

Beyond the infernal screams

From there my freedom gleamed

Returning Light

I pull over in a lay-by

Nobody is nearby

The only thing separating me from the mountain

Is the forest

And I promise

I'll be back soon

Once I've been to the summit

And touched The Moon

But on my way back

I'll bring you a gift from the night

A pocket full of fireflies

To douse you in light

Gaze

We gaze at the skies

For we love to survive

We wonder and long

About where we came from

The Universe lingers

At our fingertips

So we build ships

To traverse the great expanse

So we can expand upon

Where we come from

Amid this cosmic dance

Purpose

We're evolving into the future

We're growing from the past

We have roots but not an anchor

Or know how long time lasts

But we do have a purpose

A passion coursing through our hearts

To ever better our presence

With a timeless love that stands apart

Smile

Your smile is pure

And can be the cure

For almost everything

Go up to a mirror

Or gaze in the river

To see the truth within

It holds so much power

You can feel it devour

The fear inside

So let it empower

And bloom like a flower

Smile oh so wide

Sparkle

Our planetary feelings

Can separate us from the ceiling

Of a Universe of stars

We see them so distant

But really they're not far

In fact they glow

Inside our souls

They are our ancestors

Sparkling across space

So let's sparkle too

As one beautiful race

Traverse

I have sailed all over your heart

Yet your ocean still calls to me

So I will keep my sails aloft

And traverse you for eternity

Swathes

These saltiest of waters

And tidal swathes

That heave our capsules

Yet we persist

To sail these waves

In the hope we don't capsize

With teary dreams of treasure

In a stiff sea breeze

When we reach land

These streams pour from our eyes

Entrust

We are the beginning and the end

The flames of existence empowered

A cosmic intention

Just like the insects and the flowers

Under blazing night skies

We see the stars cry

Reminding all that they are us

The power they have given freely

Now ours to entrust

Forest of Freedom

I tamed the beast that was inside me

And found my freedom in the forest

The roots that bound my mind to fear

Vanished once I realised

I was never lost

I was merely meandering

Amongst the negative thoughts

So I swept them beneath the leaves

For them to sink beneath the soil

And now I dance in happiness

Letting my love uncoil

Fruition

Our transition

Comes to fruition

When we can listen

To the beat of our heart

When we can hear the sounds of nature

Playing like a harp

When we can see all of the connections

Between all living things

That's where freedom lies

That's where life begins

Descendant

Can you feel the sensations?

Of a million generations

Coursing through your soul

The Universe's vibrations

Through time and atoms

Making you present and whole

Now here you are

A human being of humankind

A descendant of the stars

Furnace

This deep furnace burns

As we all yearn

For our place in the sky

A knowledge sometimes forgotten

That we come from the stars

Reflecting in our eyes

Ethereal magic beings

Temporarily on Planet Earth

Reaching out to stars above

The masters of rebirth

Love & Wonder

Beyond the galaxies and nebulae

There is a world not far away

It's a place quite like no other

Where beings long to discover

For they know they come from distant stars

They are capable of such love and wonder

Beyond the fears that stop them realising

Everything is their brother

United

I want to write a poem

For every generation

To tell them we are all united

As one earthly nation

No matter where you were brought up

No matter what your views

Deep down we are all the same stuff

So let's help each other on this journey

And stick together like glue

Spirit

Do what you must

In your soul do trust

Inside the phantasm of you

Aware of the spirit so true

Blend with what you love outside

Filter out the hate and lies

Live in love with warmth so pure

Absorbing all the charm and allure

Length & Breadth

I saw the coil unravel

And knew that all outside

Is seen intrinsically

From form to shade

And thin to wide

Shape and depth

The length and breadth

So I wrote my name into the sun

And sought my path inside

Back to where I begun

Carved from tears once wept

Stratosphere

We burst through the stratosphere

Leaving Earth to explore darkness

Searching for secrets so dear

In hope for eternal answers

We ride the swirls

Of cosmic storms

To reach unimaginable destinations

And unite our souls and forms

Let Go

It all comes down to this

You must let go of fear

And embrace the bliss

That emanates freely from your heart

Allow unwanted thoughts to depart

And with your woes released

The waves of joy

Will flow into the empty space

Filling you with peace

Praise

We can be more

So much more

Beyond the lies

Of fear and scorn

We can learn to praise

And lift each other's spirits

To be the best of humanity

Unlocking all our love

To everyone that's born

Shelter

I want to take you back to the start

Show you what's within your hearts

Protect you from the fear that clouds your days

Give you shelter from the negative thoughts

That pretend they're important

Hold your hand as we learn our ways

To give you hope of a better world

One where differences don't matter

A home where we get along always

Revolution

We are the real article

A formation of particles

With a sprinkle of mutation

And a little evolution

We've become the thinkers

The ponderers and feelers

With our next logical step

A global inner revolution

One Big Family

We were built for evolving

Whilst the Earth keeps revolving

To pass our knowledge on

To sing our song

Of existence

So let's keep striving

To do more than just survive

Let us be one big family

And hold each other's hands

For eternity

Lessons

Open up the skies

And send me heavenly rain

To wash away the scourge and pain

So nothing is the same again

Let me learn lessons in the thunder

And be the bringer of storms myself

Let my lightning wake the masses

And let the floods of love remain

Kin

The only thing I see when I close my eyes

Is everything

When I sit here in the silence

I hear the cosmos sing

And the only thing I wish for you

Is to hear this too

And to see the truth

That you are one with the Universe

For we are all its kin

Fly Free

Before you drift into the darkness

I beg of you to shine your light

So your presence will always linger on

Like a star shining so bright

And when you fly free like a bird

You'll remain here in our hearts

I promise we'll cherish every moment

Before it's our turn to depart

Reminisce

Imagine you are very old
Looking back on life
Sitting in your rocking chair
Thinking what, if and why?
That for me would be heartbreaking
Because there's no rewind
To do the things you wish you'd done
In your little piece of time
So grab your life and live your dreams
It's yours after all
Don't let anybody stop you
And get up if you fall
Don't let anything hold you back
For you're alive, breathing and living
And spend this time enjoying everything
Because life will keep on giving
So you can sit in your rocking chair
When you're old and grey
Knowing you didn't waste your life
Because you lived for every day

You Are Everything

You are The Moon

You are The Sun

You are the planets far flung

You are the stars above

The fish in the ocean

The birds up in the trees

The waves of emotion

You are the leaves of autumn

And the flowers of spring

You are the invisible connections

Yes, you are everything

Find Andrew Hawkins on social media at:

Twitter @BeardedUniverse

www.facebook.com/AndrewHawkinsAuthor

www.instagram.com/andrew_hawkins_author

If you enjoyed this book please check out my other books:

Everything's Within

Vastitudes

Printed in Great Britain
by Amazon